The Evolution of Video Games

A Deep Dive into Virtual Reality Gaming

Table of Contents

I just wish the world was twice as big and half of it was still unexplored.

Chapter 1. Introduction

Immerse yourself in our gripping Special Report: "The Evolution of Video Games: A Deep Dive into Virtual Reality Gaming". Whether you are a seasoned gamer, casually feign interest or working in the tech industry, you will be both educated and amazed as we traverse the annals of gaming history and chart a course into the intriguing and boundless realms of virtual reality. This report is not merely a walk down memory lane but also a leap into the uncanny world of VR gaming, encapsulating its riveting possibilities and profound potential impacts. Guaranteed to be a journey as engaging as the games themselves, this special report will surely propel your understanding of gaming into an entirely new dimension. So, gear up and get ready to delve deep into the wild, wonderful, and wirelessly weird world of virtual reality gaming!

Chapter 2. Setting the Stage: A Concise History of Video Games

It begins, as it must, in a void of all but possibility - the mid-20th century, a time bristling with the dream of technological progress post-World War II. As mammoth computers began to be domesticated into research institutions and university laboratories, their potential for more than mere calculation and data processing started to become apparent.

2.1. The Dawn of a New Era

Indeed, the first known video game - a proto-pong game titled "Tennis for Two" - was played on an oscilloscope by physicist William Higinbotham at the Brookhaven National Laboratory in 1958. It intoxicatingly debuted the concept of manipulating visual data for entertainment, a novel idea that would eventually cascade into the immense stream of diverse electronic games we consume today.

Further ignition in this field occurred with the creation of 'Spacewar!' invented in 1962 by Steve Russell, a member of the Tech Model Railroad Club at the Massachusetts Institute of Technology. It was the first recognized game designed for computer play, making full use of the advances and processing horsepower these machines were capable of. Though limited - being text-based and played on huge mainframe computers - this early game was prophetic of the digital deluge that was to come.

2.2. The Rise of Arcade Games

Arcade games soon followed, establishing themselves as a cultural mainstay by the early 1970s. The release of Atari's Pong in 1972 brought gaming into public life, providing a taste of digital competition to wide-eyed youths at pizza parlors and bowling alleys across America. The remarkable success of Pong heralded video gaming as a budding entertainment industry, and it wasn't long before more innovative arcade games surged into the fray, dotting the neon landscape of a liberating decade with classics like 'Space Invaders', 'Pac-Man', and 'Donkey Kong'.

2.3. Commodification and the Birth of Home Consoles

Meanwhile, in tandem with the burgeoning arcade phenomenon, an equally significant revolution was taking place within the secluded comforts of the home. Ralph Baer's "Brown Box," the forerunner to the Magnavox Odyssey, was the first home video game console which brought a minimalistic form of gaming onto the television screens in 1972. The inclusion of a multiplayer feature and interchangeable game cartridges made the "Brown Box" a trailblazer in the industry.

This advent prepared the stage for the colossal entry of Atari and its iconic '2600' console in 1977, which massively popularized home gaming. Atari's high-impact entry marked the beginning of the era of home console gaming in earnest, bringing renowned characters and franchises like 'Space Invaders' and eventually 'Pac-Man' into living rooms across the world.

2.4. The Nintendo Era and the Dawn of Japanese Dominance

As the 1980s unfolded, the curtain was raised for an influential newcomer from Japan - Nintendo. Its 'NES' (Nintendo Entertainment System), launched in 1985, revitalized an industry in crisis post-

1983's video game crash, introducing unforgettable characters like Mario in the 'Super Mario Bros.' series, the adventurous Link in 'The Legend of Zelda', and the quirky aliens in 'Metroid'. These characters and narratives transformed gaming, creating a multi-dimensional framework and more extended narratives that seized the minds of millions globally.

Sega soon followed in Nintendo's footsteps with the Genesis (or 'Mega-Drive' as known in some regions) in 1988, offering compelling franchises like 'Sonic the Hedgehog'. The rivalry between Sega and Nintendo encapsulated the fervor of 90s gaming, driving massive leaps in quality, content, and technological advancement.

Taken together, these various chapters from the historical annals of video games provide us with a rich basis for understanding the trajectory of the industry. From the humble stirrings within laboratories to the deluge of arcade classics, followed by the advent of home consoles and the Japanese drive that solidified gaming as a fixture of popular culture, it truly was a journey laced with technological marvels and unanticipated leaps. As we progress into deeper layers of this report, we shall continue to reference this history and its vital lessons. Yet, as compelling as the past is, it is in the thrilling future where the most incredible potentials lie, as we shall soon discover. Now, let's venture forth!

Chapter 3. Understanding the Basics: The Anatomy of a Video Game

From the early days of Pong, Space Invaders, and Pac-Man, the gaming industry has undergone a seismic evolution, forging a path from simplistic 2D monochrome games to today's immersive, hyper-realistic 3D worlds. The intricacy of these games' mechanics and their applications are unprecedented in the history of entertainment mediums. By delving into the anatomy of these masterpieces, we can gain a deeper understanding and appreciation of the game-making craft - an art and science in its own right.

3.1. Pixels, Polygons, and Processing Power

At its most basic, a video game is an interactive digital simulation operating on electronic systems, colloquially termed as platforms. These platforms can range from home consoles, handheld consoles, arcade machines, computers, mobile devices, or even VR headsets. The game software instructs these systems to generate sound and visuals that provide an engaging and fulfilling entertainment experience to the user.

Video games are synergistically composed of two key components: graphics and sound, each intricately structured to provide an immersive playing environment. The graphics make extensive use of pixels and polygons while the sounds - both music and sound effects - are meticulously designed to match the action and mood of the game.

Arguably, the pebble upon which this digital mosaic is built is the pixel. Compounded from 'picture' and 'element', each pixel represents a minute area on the screen. Color information is encoded into pixels, which are strategically organized and manipulated to form a larger composition - the game world. On the other hand, three-dimensional games use polygons to construct models and build virtual environments. A polygon, commonly a triangle in the context of game design, functions as the basic building block to create complex 3D objects and structures.

The device responsible for rendering these pixels and polygons is the Graphics Processing Unit (GPU). Working in tandem with the Central Processing Unit (CPU), the GPU generates images by decoding the software's instructions into electrical signals sent to the display device, creating the game's visuals.

Parallel to the evolution of graphics, game sound designs have advanced remarkably. From simple bleeps and bloops in early games, we now have orchestral scores and realistic sound effects recorded in hi-fidelity audio. The combination of advanced sound and visual design enriches the overall gaming experience.

3.2. Input and Interaction

Another vital aspect of video games is input and interaction, the bridge between the player and the game. This typically involves the use of a controller, joystick, keyboard, mouse, or touchscreen. The system receives player input as electronic signals, translating them into in-game actions. Over the years, these inputs have evolved immensely, now including voice commands and gesture-based controls, thus expanding the avenues of player interaction.

So, how does this work? The process begins with input devices like gamepads or motion controls detecting the player's actions, converting these into electrical impulses which are then sent to the system. The game's engine, considered its 'brain', interprets these signals, triggering appropriate responses in the game's state. This entire process is executed in a split second, ensuring an immersive and responsive gameplay experience.

3.3. The Game Engine: The Heart of Video Games

At the heart of every game lies a game engine, the core software component on which games run. This engine coordinates everything within the game, including physics, graphics, audio, AI behavior, and even player input.

Within the game engine, game physics mimics real or imagined physical properties, such as gravity, collision responses or fluid dynamics, creating a distinct, plausible environment for the player to engage with. Equally important is the Engine's AI module where the behaviour of non-player characters (NPCs) is scripted, making them responsive to player actions and evolving game dynamics, creating increasingly lifelike and challenging interaction scenarios.

Finally, let's explore the concept of game states. In essence, a game state signifies the current condition or circumstances of the game at any given time. Elements contributing to the game state could include character positions, collected items, enemy health, unlocked levels, and much more. These states are constantly updated through the game engine to reflect the current status and progress within the game.

3.4. Conclusion

With a glimpse into the intricate anatomy of a video game, we can now better appreciate the complexity hidden behind the engrossing worlds our screens display. This understanding allows us not just to grasp the deeper intricacies of our favourite games, but also equips us to anticipate and value the evolutions that the gaming industry continually offers us. Whether you're a game developer, a dedicated gamer, or a curious bystander, understanding these basics illuminates the intricate artistry and engineering behind the games that captivate us, setting the stage for the exploration of the thrilling world of 3D and VR gaming that lies ahead.

Chapter 4. The Shift to 3D Gaming: A Revolution in the Making

Our journey through the fascinating panorama of video game history leads us to a critical juncture— the epochal shift from 2D to 3D gaming. This monumental development can be well considered as nothing short of a revolution in the gaming industry, delivering a seismic impact on how game developers conceptualized games and how players engaged with them. The shift didn't happen overnight, though. It summoned the combined forces of technological advancements, innovative game design, and the ceaseless aspiration to create more immersive gaming environments.

4.1. The Dawn of 3D Gaming

The first wind of change blew in the late 1980s with games such as "Elite", released in 1984, employing wireframe 3D graphics. In essence, these were simple renditions of 3D объект using crosshatches to represent solid areas. To say they were primitive by today's standard would be an understatement, but it was a stepping stone that set the stage for what was yet to come.

A more nuanced approach toward 3D gaming appeared in 1986 with games like "The Sentinel" and "Star Luster." These iconic titles provided the first dynamic 3D experiences. Cartesian coordinates were used to render the game's environment and assets in three dimensions, allowing users to cruise around and navigate in a virtual 3D space.

4.2. Advancements in Hardware

The jump from 2D to 3D would not have been possible without significant advancements in hardware. In particular, the development of the GPU (Graphical Processing Unit) was a game-changer. First seen with the Sega Model 1 in 1992, the GPU provided hardware acceleration for rendering 3D graphics, shifting the rendering load away from the CPU.

By 1993, ATi and S3 were producing dedicated graphics cards for PC gaming, launching a heated competition that would fuel exponential advancements in graphics processing. Computers and consoles started incorporating faster chips, enabling developers to create smooth frame rates with fewer distortions and to create objects with more polygons.

Fundamental to the 3D revolution was the fifth generation of video game consoles, namely the Sony PlayStation, Sega Saturn, and Nintendo 64. They debuted during the mid-1990s, offering graphical capabilities that surpassed earlier consoles, with a focus on 3D graphics.

4.3. The Rise of 3D in Software

While hardware improvements certainly accelerated the shift to 3D, the relentless creativity and ambition of developers played a massive part too. Polygon rendering was a crucial early innovation, with games like "Virtua Fighter" (1993) and "Doom" (1993) leveraging this method to create characters and environments with an unprecedented level of depth and nuance.

The fully textured, 3D polygon graphics became prominent with games like "Super Mario 64" and "The Legend of Zelda: Ocarina of Time" on the Nintendo 64. These games were not merely about impressive visual enhancements, but they also created entirely novel and immersive gameplay mechanics, which made full use of the expansive, explorable 3D space.

The trending approach was to couple advanced hardware with innovative software that manipulated polygons and applied textures to them, creating impressively realistic imagery for the time. Game developers embraced this shift as they explored the potential of this nascent technology to offer players a new dimension in interactive experiences.

4.4. The Implications of the 3D Revolution

Looking beyond the technical aspects, the shift to 3D gaming had unprecedented implications for gamers and the broader industry. It fundamentally redefined the way players interacted with games. In 2D platforms, the gamer's viewpoint was limited, but the advent of 3D environments opened up fresh paradigms of interaction. The sense of agency and immersion this provided, helped to broaden the appeal of gaming to a wider audience.

For the gaming industry, the shift was equal parts exciting and challenging, pushing them to adapt to these evolving demands. Businesses began investing heavily in R & D and operations, while programmers learned to harness the power of new programming languages.

The revolution stretched out into the decades that followed, with continuous refinement and reinvention of 3D gaming technology. In particular, the rise of Virtual Reality (VR) and Augmented Reality (AR) gaming were only made possible thanks to the solid foundation built during the 3D gaming revolution.

The period of the 1990s was a time of disruption and innovation in the world of video games. The stage was set for the next sector-altering shift – the advent of the internet and the connectivity it endowed, leading to a rise in multiplayer online gaming. This storyline tells us, from a distinctive vantage point, how software's persistent evolution tends to shape and be shaped by the ceaseless march of hardware advancements.

So, let's move onwards with our voyage into the universe of gaming, packing with us the insights we've derived from looking at this crucial phase of transition and transformation in the gaming world.

Chapter 5. The Internet Impact: How Connectivity Changed Gaming

The advent of the internet has truly transformed and reshaped the world in unimaginable ways. Its tendrils have reached into virtually every corner of human existence, and the realm of gaming is no stranger to its definitive impact. The seismic shift in gaming due to the advent of connectivity remains an epic saga that tells a tale of bridging gaps and fostering unity in an otherwise divided world.

5.1. The Dawn of Internet Connectivity in Gaming

In the beginning, video games were solitary experiences, limited by the technical constraints of their time. Whether they were home console games or computer games, the modus operandi was simple: players would pit their wits against a preprogrammed computer opponent, or battle for high scores in a ceaseless retreat from impending virtual doom - essentially, a single-player experience.

Just as the first rays of sunlight illuminate a landscape, illuminating unseen hues and casting new shadows, the inception of internet connectivity shone a new light onto the gaming landscape. The earliest inklings of this shift were seen in the late 1970s, with games like 'MUD1' (Multi-User Dungeon) and 'Adventure', manifestations of the revolutionary concept of multiplayer gaming over the internet. It was a shift that extended the horizon of possibility, allowing for richer narratives, imaginative gameplay mechanics and interactive experiences on scales previously unimaginable.

5.2. Multiplayer Gaming and Massive Multiplayer Online Role-Playing Games (MMORPGs)

The widespread cultivation of internet connectivity brought forth a novel concept of gaming: the multiplayer universe. Multiplayer games pitted players against one another, no longer against a processed sequence of 1s and 0s. This revolutionized video games, transforming them into a social experience. New genres emerged, such as strategy games, where connectivity allowed players to compete or cooperate, forging new alliances and bitter rivalries.

The inception of multiplayer gaming was later succeeded by the phenomenon of Massive Multiplayer Online Role-Playing Games (MMORPGs). Titles such as 'World of Warcraft' and 'Final Fantasy XI' captivated audiences worldwide, offering immersive fantasy-filled worlds where untold thousands could interact, quest, and explore together in real-time. They were digital microcosms operating on live, fluctuating economies governed by player actions. In essence, they were near-tangible reflections of society within a virtual framework.

5.3. The Introduction of Online Gaming Platforms

Just as every kingdom requires a sturdy castle, every online game needs a reliable platform. Gaming companies acknowledged this and sought to provide ecosystems that could host these digital experiences. Online gaming platforms such as Xbox Live, PlayStation Network, and Steam, revolutionized the way games were distributed, played and updated. They not only hosted multiplayer games but also served as digital marketplaces. It led to the rise of digital downloads, shifting the paradigm away from physical copies of games. The platforms also allowed for real-time updates and patches, leading to a gaming culture where games could evolve and grow post-release.

5.4. The Rise of Competitive Gaming and Esports

The world has always loved competition. From gladiator fights in Roman colosseums to the World Cup, competitive events have ultimately stood the test of time. With connectivity came the capacity for competition, and thus, the arena of eSports was born. Competitive gaming exploded onto the scene with leagues, tournaments and professional players; it was no longer a mere hobby, but an established, legitimate sport. Games like 'Starcraft', 'Dota 2', and 'League of Legends' garnered mass viewership, and their competitive landscapes cultivated a new branch of entertainment that was as thrilling to watch as traditional sports.

5.5. The Impact on Game Design and Development

The introduction of internet connectivity has had profound repercussions on the game development process as well. Designers and developers now had to contemplate the online component while designing games, considering not just a player, but a community of players. Concepts of online cooperation and competition, economy systems, and multiplayer mechanics became a foundation over which many games were built.

5.6. Societal and Economic Implications

Online connectivity in games also brought with it societal changes;

gamers were no longer stereotyped as loners in their basements but became part of growing international communities. On the economic front, the new business models, digital distribution and in-game purchases provided a consistent revenue stream for developers and publishers.

In conclusion, the story of how internet connectivity changed gaming is a tumultuous tale of advancements and transformations. It has upended old norms, given rise to new horizons, and reshaped the gaming landscape irrevocably. A once solitary hobby has evolved into a connective experience that unites millions worldwide. As we peer into the future, we can only anticipate what the continued advancements within the realm of technology have in store for gaming. Regardless of which games we play, it is indisputable that the internet has turned gaming into an evolving, dynamic form of enthralling interactive entertainment.

Chapter 6. Intro to Virtual Reality: Immersion, Interaction, Innovation

Before we delve deep into the world of Virtual Reality (VR), it's essential to understand precisely what VR refers to. Often depicted in popular culture as an esoteric blend of reality and matrix, VR is a remarkable technique for creating a simulated environment that can be interacted with in a seemingly real or physical way. This immersive technology tricks our brains into accepting the virtual world as part of reality by employing multidimensional, high-quality audio-visual factors and other sensory cues.

6.1. The Intricacies of Immersion

Undeniably, virtual reality immersion is among the key characteristics of VR that distinguishes it from more traditional gaming experiences. In VR, 'immersion' refers to the sensation of being completely enveloped or engrossed in the virtual environment, producing a visceral disconnect from the actual physical surroundings. This sense of immersion is achieved through a combination of complex and innovative hardware and software systems.

Primarily, the hardware involved in creating immersive VR experiences includes Head-Mounted Displays (HMDs), motion trackers, haptic feedback devices, and VR controllers or gloves. These devices collaborated to generate two crucial enrichments for immersion - a convincing field of view and accurate, real-time tracking of player's movements. Remarkably, these devices reproduce real-world physics within the VR environment, thus enhancing the immersion further.

Furthermore, high-resolution graphics and sophisticated sound design are integral parts of the immersion process. Visually, VR applications must render realistic environments with a high field of view, and the power to do so hinges on the graphical capabilities of the platform. Sound design, on the other hand, takes advantage of spatial or 3D audio – sound that seems to come from a specific location within the environment.

6.2. The Importance of Interaction

Interaction in VR reshapes the established principles of player engagement found in traditional video games, fostering a deeper and more intimate connection between the player and the virtual world. It offers an essentially active experience, requiring gestures, movements, and other physical interactions from the player, therefore extending the gaming experience into the tangible realm.

A crucial element of VR interaction design is the user interface (UI). Unlike conventional video games that largely rely on 2D menus and text boxes, VR games necessitate interfaces that are integrated seamlessly into the 3D game world, ensuring they do not disrupt the sense of immersion. This approach paved the way to gaze-based interaction, proximity interaction, and direct manipulation, which are now standard in many VR systems.

Given that VR encourages kinaesthetic engagement, haptic feedback gains exponential significance. Haptic technology in VR interfaces affords users the ability to 'feel' or 'touch' virtual objects, creating a novel tactile layer of interaction. From the subtle vibration of a controller to more advanced haptic suits that simulate physical impacts, the potential this technology holds is tremendous.

6.3. A Glimpse into Innovation

When it comes to innovation, VR leads from the front in the gaming industry. It challenges traditional design paradigms and ushers in unique gameplay mechanisms, narratives, and aesthetics that have never been explored in the confines of conventional gaming.

One particularly intriguing form of innovation is the concept of 'presence', the psychological sense of 'being there' in the virtual environment. Games can induce this feeling of presence using numerous tricks, such as spatial audio that reacts to the player's position and direction, intuitive interaction systems, lifelike animations, and a consistent 'reality' within the game world.

Moreover, the breakthrough realm of social VR adds another level of dynamism to the equation. With multi-user capabilities, online VR environments are burgeoning social and gaming spaces where interaction goes beyond the game mechanics, encompassing communication with other players, shared experiences, collaborative gameplay, and player-driven narratives.

Innovation stretches beyond the gameplay experiences to aspects of game development as well. Designing for VR has sparked new methodologies in concepts like 'user-centered design' and 'iterative prototyping', given the unique challenges and opportunities that VR presents.

In essence, the vivid world of virtual reality gaming, complete with its immersion, interaction, and innovation, provides an unparalleled evolution in interactive entertainment. As we explore the dynamics of VR further in this report, one can only imagine what awe-inspiring facets are yet to be unveiled in the enthralling leap from traditional gaming to the extraordinarily immersive virtual reality gaming.

Chapter 7. The Devices that Drive VR: An Overview of Key Hardware

Our journey into the captivating world of virtual reality (VR) gaming cannot proceed without understanding the machinery that underpins this universe. The hardware is the physical interface that bridges the gap between our reality and the virtual planes of existence within the games we immerse ourselves in. In this chapter, we shall dissect the essential components of VR hardware subsuming headsets, controllers, sensors and accompanying accessories, while elucidating their role in establishing an immersive VR gaming experience.

7.1. The Crown Jewel: VR Headsets

A VR headset is a head-mounted device that provides virtual reality for the wearer. It is the main gateway into the virtual world, comparable to a window that opens to a vibrant and interactive expanse, which you are a part of.

Not all headsets are manufactured equal. There are primarily two categories: tethered and standalone. Tethered headsets, like the Oculus Rift or the HTC Vive, are physically connected to PCs and tend to offer a more visually impressive and responsive experience. These devices wield the power of the PC to run advanced VR games.

Standalone headsets, such as Oculus Quest, offer a different proposition. Here, you discover the freedom of wireless gaming; they contain all necessary components within the headset itself. They might not provide the graphical prowess of tethered headsets, but the ease of use and mobility make them a strong contender for mainstream adoption.

Each headset is equipped with a screen (or two) displaying the game environment. It applies stereoscopic displays to offer a three-dimensional perception. In addition, sensors embedded in the device keep track of the player's movements and adjust the visual display accordingly.

7.2. In The Palms Of Your Hands: Controllers and Haptic Devices

Controllers are akin to physical manifestations of your hands within the virtual landscape; they are the conduits through which you interact with the virtual environment.

Early VR controllers copied traditional gaming peripherals. The evolution, however, has escalated to advanced contraptions that can track positional movements along with the orientation. The Valve Index controllers, for instance, not only track the position of your hands but also detect the individual movements of your fingers, thus allowing for greater control and immersion.

Haptic feedback devices, another significant breakthrough, provide tactile sensations simulating the feel of objects in the game, offering a depth to the sense of immersion and realism. From the vibrations of a controller mimicking the recoil of a gun to more sophisticated glove-like devices that can recreate the sensation of touch, haptic technology widens the scope of immersive gaming.

7.3. Reading the Room: Sensors and Tracking Systems

Sensors and tracking systems form the backbone of the VR experience. They monitor the player's movements and translate them into in-game actions.

Prominent tracking systems include outside-in and inside-out tracking. Outside-in tracking, as seen in early versions of HTC Vive, involves external sensors placed in the room to track your movements. Inside-out tracking, found in Oculus Rift S and Oculus Quest, uses sensors on the headset itself to read the environment and follow the player's movements.

Both methods have their strengths: where outside-in tracking delivers precise tracking, inside-out offers improved convenience with no need for external sensors.

7.4. The Unsung Heroes: Audio Devices

Audio gears play a vital part in enriching the VR experience. Spatial audio, also known as 3D audio, crucially complements the visual immersion with acoustic immersion. This technology creates a sound environment that realistically mimics how we experience sound in the real world. When done right, you can sense the direction of footsteps, the distant hum of an engine, or the close whisper of an ally, heightening the perception of being "inside" the game.

7.5. Accompanying Accessories

Lastly, let us not forget about the myriad of accessories available. While not essential, these add-ons can elevate the VR experience. Ranging from omnidirectional treadmills for realistic locomotion to VR suits providing full-body haptic feedback, the selection is steadily growing, further erasing the line between virtuality and reality.

Through our exploration of the devices that drive VR, we realize that while the graphics are what we see, the hardware is what we truly experience. It defines the parameters of interaction with our virtual environment, grounds us into the beautifully coding-built worlds, and thereafter, becomes an essential part of propulsion into the ethereal expanses of virtual reality. Yes, they are built of wires, screens, and sensors but in essence, they hold the keys to experiences yet untamed, narratives yet unfurled, and dimensions yet unexplored.

Chapter 8. Content in Context: A Look at VR Gaming Genres

The universe of virtual reality is one that is unendingly expansive, intricate and multidimensional. When VR meets the fascinating realm of gaming, the result is a plethora of genres that cater to every type of gamer. A dive into the genres of VR gaming does not simply involve a breakdown of different types but requires understanding the immersive experience each genre seeks to provide and the context in which the genre and its content operate.

8.1. An Overview of VR Gaming Genres

Our journey into the depths of VR gaming genres would be incomplete without stepping into multiple virtual landscapes. There is a multitude of game genres. By exploring a selection of them, we can begin to understand the limitless potential of VR gaming and its ability to surpass boundaries and transcend our normal reality. Every genre, though different, is united by a common goal: to fully immerse players in a virtual world that reacts and responds to their actions.

1. Adventure: Encouraging exploration and problem-solving, adventure games take players on epic quests in expansive, detailed environments. Employing intricate storylines and complex puzzles, these games offer a fully interactive 3D experience. Examples include "The Gallery - Episode 1: Call of the Starseed" and "Moss."

2. First-person shooters (FPS): Known for their exhilarating action,

first-person shooters in VR take the adrenaline-packed experience to a new level by truly placing the player in the heat of battle. Titles like "Onward" and "Pavlov VR" are known for their realistic weapon handling.

3. Music and Rhythm: Players become performers in these games, keeping time and rhythm with the music. Beat Saber, an iconic title, has players slashing beats in vibrant neon lights.

4. Educational: These can range from history games transporting players to ancient civilizations, to medical simulations that allow for VR surgeries. "Apollo 11 VR" lets players witness man's first journey to the moon.

5. Sports: By simulating real-world physical activities, these games provide an active, exhilarating alternative to traditional sports. Games like "The Climb" and "Echo Arena" use VR's immersive capabilities to their full potential.

8.2. Immersion, Interactivity and Genre Specifics

What makes each VR genre unique is the immersion and interactivity it offers. In the world of VR gaming, a genre is more than just a category—it's a carefully designed, immersive experience that strives to transport gamers into an alternate reality.

When we take a look at adventure games, for instance, they truly redefine the term 'interactive storytelling'. These games often focus on narratives and plots, often taking the form of quests or journeys. They leverage the VR system's capabilities to make players feel like they are physically navigating a virtual world, solving puzzles, and interacting with characters, creating a genuine sense of presence. An adventurous game in VR is more than just visually stunning—it is also about vibrant characters, intricate plots, and the unimaginable becoming real right in front of you.

With first-person shooter games, the defining characteristic is arguably the increased level of immersion. These games strive to create a particularly visceral, combat-oriented experience for users, giving them the ability to hold weapons, aim, fire, and perform defensive maneuvers. The three-dimensional space that VR offers further enhances the player's sense of control, creating the feeling of actually being in a combat scenario in a way that traditional video games simply cannot replicate.

Educational VR games are an entirely different ball game. They use the immersive and interactive strengths of VR to create coursewares that enhance learning. Through first-hand experiences, VR educational games can provide insights into complex topics in a way that textbooks often fail. A journey through space or an underwater exploration of the Great Barrier Reef become vivid, unforgettable experiences that enrich understanding far more than any traditional teaching method could.

8.3. The Art and Implication of Design in VR Gaming Genres

Visual design elements and aesthetics play a critical role in VR gaming. Games need to be visually engaging to maintain a player's attention. They require carefully crafted environments, characters, and objects full of life and depth. Adding to this, the specific requirements of VR—such as the need to prevent motion sickness—mean that game designers must deliberate over each design decision with care.

Designers often need to carry out user testing to achieve a balance between realism and comfort. It is important to note that realism in VR does not always correlate with increased immersion. Sometimes too much realism can lead to players experiencing virtual reality sickness, similar to motion sickness. The goal, therefore, is to create a visually pleasing and immersive world that players could believably inhabit, whilst minimizing discomfort and illness.

8.4. The Future of VR Gaming Genres

Looking ahead, the future of VR gaming genres seems nothing short of awe-inspiring. As VR technology continues to advance, we will witness genres blending and expanding in intriguing ways. There are discussions about utilizing AI to elevate the role of non-playable characters (NPCs), making them more realistic and dynamic. This implies that the AI would react to players in different ways based on their actions, leading to infinite gameplay possibilities. Another gripping area researchers are focusing on is haptic feedback, which engages our sense of touch, further amplifying immersion.

With the ongoing advancements of VR, it is not a wild guess that in the coming years, we will witness the creation of new genres that we can't even fathom today. The exploration of VR gaming genres gives us a glimpse into the uncharted waters of a brave new world of gaming, that breaks away from flat screens and controllers to bring us a form of entertainment that truly immerses and excites.

The journey into virtual reality gaming genres hence demonstrates the staggering breadth and depth of the VR gaming world. Each genre, with its own special characteristics and specific design requirements, provides a different way to experience new realities. The potential for unforeseen genres to emerge as the technology evolves is a testament to the boundless capabilities of VR. The curtain is truly rising on an expansive new era in gaming, and we are all invited to partake in it.

Chapter 9. Unleashing Imagination: The Design and Development of VR Games

Right at the heart of the world of virtual reality (VR) gaming is the design and development of these virtual landscapes and experiences. The creation of VR games requires not just a profound understanding of conventional game development, but also a deep immersion into the unique capacities and limitations of VR technology. This is a domain defined by ceaseless innovation, constant iteration, and unending imagination. It's where the borders of reality begin to blur and the canvas of creativity is as expansive as a developer's vision.

9.1. Approach to VR Game Design

The approach to VR game design entails a profound paradigm shift from traditional video game design. Unlike traditional games that necessitate a certain detachment from the gaming environment, VR is all about creating immersive systems that completely encapsulate the players within the virtual world, offering them direct agency and interaction.

The crux of VR game design lies in this immediacy and immersion combined with intuitiveness. Developers have to handle numerous aesthetic, technical and experiential aspects meticulously to ensure seamless and natural interactions. These require a detailed understanding of spatial audio, stereoscopic vision, and motion controls among others.

9.2. Spatial Design in VR Games

VR spatial design is fundamentally about designing an interactive three-dimensional (3D) environment that is engaging, evocative, and comfortable for players to navigate. The challenge is not just to construct enticing visuals, but to weave environmental storytelling and interactive mechanics cooperatively together to forge a coherent and absorbing experience.

Player orientation and ease of navigation must be prioritized, lest players suffer from disorientation or discomfort during play. Careful consideration of the play space's scale and size is crucial, planning the deployment of environmental objects, and designing movement systems that aren't likely to induce simulation sickness.

9.3. Narrative Design and Player Agency

In VR games, narrative design has an additional layer of complexity due to the increased level of player agency. As the player controls a first-person perspective within a 3D environment, the narrative unfolds around them in a simultaneous and spatial manner, often creating multiple branching paths of story development.

Designers in VR have a unique ability to craft intriguing, non-linear narratives that allow players to interact and engage more directly, resulting in a deeper emotional connection and personalized experiences. However, maintaining narrative coherence while allowing for considerable player agency is an art that VR developers must master, necessitating profound creativity, skill, and often, innovative thinking.

9.4. Technical Consideration in VR Development

[A] Motion Control: VR game development requires taking motion control into account. Developers must leverage the 6 degrees of freedom (6DoF) that VR hardware provides to design controls that are instinctive and responsive. For example, utilizing the motion-tracking capabilities of VR for freehand interactions with objects in the game world vastly improves the sense of immersion and agency for a player.

[B] Audio: Spatial audio is a key aspect of immersion in VR. Simply put, sounds must come from the correct direction and shift as the player moves. VR developers must ensure that spatial sound design syncs with graphics to create a unified, immersive experience.

[C] Performance: VR game development also requires optimization at a level far beyond regular video games. They must maintain a high, stable frame rate and low latency to prevent discomfort, nausea, or motion sickness among players.

9.5. The Process of VR Game Development

The process of VR game development is iterative and requires multidisciplinary expertise—it runs the gamut from concept artists, 3D modellers, animators, sound designers to programmers, and even psychologists. It starts with preproduction, where the game concept, mechanics, aesthetics, and narrative are defined and storyboarded.

From there, a small vertical slice of the game is developed to assess the feasibility and fun factor of the intended design. Based on the feedback collected, iterative prototyping is carried out, with repeated cycles of testing, feedback, and improvement. This cycle continues until the game matches the vision of the designers and delights the players all while staying within the constraints of the technology.

Once the prototype is green-lit, full production ensues, and assets are finalized, levels are built, and the game is gradually pieced together. After sufficient testing for both bugs and user experience, the game is then released—but the work doesn't end there. Post-release, developers need to ensure they provide support and updates to their end-users, fixing bugs, adding content, and refining gameplay based on player feedback.

The design and development of VR games are a magnificent blend of science, technology, art, and psychology. It fuses creativity with complex algorithms, breath-taking art with ground-breaking technology, and human intuition with artificial intelligence, creating vivid, vibrant virtual worlds teeming with possibility and promise. It is a testament to human imagination's vast capabilities, driving us ever further into the labyrinthine realms of simulated reality. The current state of VR gaming is simply the nascent stage of what is sure to be a thrilling journey of exploration, immersion, and more, ushering us into a future buzzing with limitless potential. The unshackling of our imaginations is just beginning in the riveting world of VR gaming.

Chapter 10. Navigating Through Impacts: The Social, Psychological, and Economic Dimensions of VR Gaming

As society is propelled into the digital age, technology has inevitably integrated into nearly every facet of our lives. The gaming industry, especially the realm of Virtual Reality (VR), is no exception. The impact of VR gaming extends far beyond the mere realm of entertainment. It traverses the social, psychological, and economic spheres, forging a transformational path impacting individuals and society on multiple levels. To clarify, in this chapter, we would discuss the various dimensions of VR gaming and how they are shaping social interactions, personal psyche and the global economy.

10.1. The Social Impact of VR Gaming

Video games have long been a conduit for social interaction. From the early days of collaborative 'Pong' to the massive-multiplayer online games (MMOs) of today, the shared experience of gaming has been pivotal to its popularity. However, the advent of VR has revolutionized this dynamic, facilitating an unprecedented level of immersive social interaction.

In VR, the user doesn't just play a character, but becomes one - interacting with the virtual world in a way that mimics real-life movements and reactions. This realism fosters a profound sense of shared experience. Users are able to communicate and cooperate with other players around the globe, erasing geographical boundaries and fostering greater cultural understanding.

However, the social implication of VR gaming is not limited to positive outcomes. There is the potential for heightened anonymity and the misuse of the same. Furthermore, there could be a blurring of boundaries between real and virtual, leading to social isolation in extreme scenarios. As such, acknowledging these potential negatives is essential for the development of responsible VR practices.

10.2. Psychological Implications of VR Gaming

The psychological implications of VR gaming are equally significant. On one hand, VR can offer therapeutic benefits. By harnessing the immersive qualities of VR, mental health practitioners can use the technology as a tool for exposure therapy, using it to recreate potentially anxiety-inducing scenarios in a safe and controlled manner to help patients tackle their fears over time.

Furthermore, VR offers developers a unique means of crafting experiences that evoke empathy and understanding. In allowing players to fully immerse themselves in the perspective of another, VR games can foster empathy for different life experiences.

Yet, like its social implications, the psychological impact of VR gaming isn't without its potential downsides. Excessive use of VR can lead to disassociation or even addiction. As VR technology continues to advance, the lines between the real and the virtual may blur, potentially causing psychological distress for some individuals. Thus, careful regulation and research into the long-term psychological effects of VR are vital.

10.3. Economic Ramifications of VR Gaming

From an economic perspective, VR gaming is ushering in a new era, not just for the gaming industry, but for technology as a whole. As of 2020, the global VR gaming market was valued at approximately $13.5 billion and it is expected to reach $92.31 billion by 2027, exhibiting a compound annual growth rate of over 30%. Its explosive growth is creating new job opportunities in VR game design, development, and marketing, among others. Additionally, its unrealistic growth is fostering further innovation in related sectors such as hardware and software development, 3D graphics, and AI, stimulating the overall technological economy.

However, the economic benefits of VR gaming extend beyond financial gains. It also serves as an educational tool, aiding students in learning a multitude of subjects from history to science in a more engaging manner. Businesses are increasingly turning to VR for training purposes, leveraging it to simulate various situations for employee training, leading to cost savings and efficiency gains.

As with any burgeoning industry, there are economic risks. These include market saturation, the high costs of VR hardware, and the potential for an economic bubble if growth outstrips the actual value of the sector. However, careful market analysis and regulation can mitigate these risks.

In conclusion, the dimensions of VR gaming are far-reaching, influencing society from social, psychological, and economic perspectives. While the positive impacts are many, there are also potential negatives that must be carefully considered and addressed. As VR continues to evolve, it is imperative for all stakeholders, from users and developers to policy makers and mental health practitioners, to engage in ongoing dialogue and research to ensure that this technology provides maximum benefits while minimizing potential harm. The journey down the road of VR gaming is undeniably exciting, but also requires careful navigation.

Chapter 11. The Future of Gaming: Emerging Trends in VR and Beyond

Immerse yourself in the adrenaline-pumping, photon-bending world of tomorrow as we stride boldly into the heart of what the future holds for gaming's most exhilarating frontier: Virtual reality.

11.1. What's Next for Virtual Reality?

As the digital clock ticks ever forward, VR gaming continues its relentless progression, affirming its place in the pantheon of technological marvels. The future appears to shimmer with promise, where the lines between the gaming world and the real world will blur so much that discerning between the two might bea challenge. We are set to unveil a wholly immersed, fully interactive, multisensory experience that invades and pervades every aspect of our perception – a truly boundary-breaking advance on an epic scale.

A significant trend that seems destined to fuel VR's future evolution is the increasing affordability of VR devices. While the technology still carries considerable cost, advances in manufacturing techniques and falling component prices are making it an increasingly accessible means of entertainment for all consumers, not just the privileged few. As more people adopt VR, the funding for R&D increases, fostering an upward spiral in both hardware sophistication and software innovation - thus perpetuating an industry-wide revolution in VR gaming.

11.2. Immersive Graphics

One aspect dominating the VR research terrains is the quest for higher resolution graphics. Today's VR headsets may produce crisp images, but future hardware aims to achieve photorealism – the holy grail of graphic design. Photorealistic graphics, combined with the encompassing vision provided by VR, would create an indistinguishable-from-reality gaming experience. Though this might seem as distant as a star in another galaxy, the advances in nanotechnology and GPU performance breed optimism for its eventual realization.

11.3. Expanding Fields of Play

Virtual reality's current core competency lies solely within the gaming realm. In the future, however, we expect to see virtual reality penetrate other areas of entertainment – cinema, music shows, sports, tourism, and even social networking are ripe for VR infiltration. Imagine attending a concert of your favorite band, navigating a Roman amphitheater, or even engaging in a virtual meet-up with friends, all from the comfort of your living room. The potential reaches far beyond gaming and extends to every sphere of entertainment.

11.4. Haptic Wonders

A significant area for VR's further evolution is haptics, the sense of touch in a digital world. Advances in haptic technology promise a future where virtual objects feel real and can be interacted with in consistent, realistic ways. Imagine donning a VR glove that not only tracks your hand movements but also simulates the texture and weight of virtual objects – the essential touch to total immersion!

11.5. AI and ML Enhancements

While advanced graphics and haptic feedback will enhance the VR gaming experience's aesthetic and sensory aspects, the future of VR might also revolutionize gameplay itself. Artificial intelligence (AI) and machine learning (ML) are set to take center stage in creating non-player characters (NPCs) that learn, adapt and evolve according to the gamer's playstyle. This dynamic environment revolutionizes the VR gaming experience, making games more immersive and unpredictable.

11.6. Cognitive Extension

The farthest frontier on VR's horizon is the cognitive extension where the headset doesn't just track head and eye movements, but also reads brain activity. By tracking the mental states of gamers, future VR systems could adjust game settings in real-time according to the user's emotions, making for genuinely personalized and immersive content.

11.7. Final Thoughts

In conclusion, the future of VR gaming is an alchemical mix of tantalizing promises and nascent potential. By making virtual worlds more affordable, realistic, and immersive, the revolutionary horizon of VR gaming could redefine what it means to play, blurring the lines between digital and reality more than ever before. What is clear is that virtual reality's future is bright and expansive, and these upcoming shifts will transform the gaming landscape in ways we can only begin to imagine. Stepping into the evolving VR gaming terrain, we find ourselves at the cusp of a new dawn, where the portal to infinite possibilities has only just begun to open. Buckle up! This ride into the future of VR gaming is bound to be exciting and unprecedented.

www.ingramcontent.com/pod-product-compliance
Lightning Source LLC
LaVergne TN
LVHW051632050326
832903LV00033B/4724